the act of OBEDIENCE

OBEDIENCE THAT COST NOTHING CHANGES NOTHING

The glory to be revealed after suffering outweighs the cost of obedience

PETER LENGWE

Printed in the United States of America

ISBN:
Softcover: 978-1-972299-24-1
Hardback   978-1-972299-25-8
eBook: 978-1-972299-23-4

For more information or ministry resources, please visit:

Peter Lengwe | THE BREAD OF LIFE GLOBAL MINISTRIES

ABOUT THE AUTHOR

Peter Lengwe is a devoted student of the Word of God, called to illuminate the timeless truths of Scripture through clear, Spirit-led teaching and heartfelt devotion. His writings are known for their depth, simplicity, and reverence — guiding readers to see the living hand of God at work throughout history and within the human heart.

Driven by a deep love for Jesus Christ and a longing to see believers walk in truth, Peter writes with both theological precision and pastoral warmth. His works invite readers to not only understand Scripture but to experience it — to live by the same faith and obedience that marked the saints of old.

Peter's first book, In the Beginning the Heavens and the Earth as Created (2022), explored the majesty of God's creation and the authority of His Word.

His second, Pierced for Our Transgressions: A Devotional and Doctrinal Journey Through the Final Days of Jesus Christ, traced the final week of the Lord's earthly ministry, revealing the redemptive perfection of His sacrifice.

In The Act of Obedience, Peter continues his calling — leading readers on a journey through the lives of God's faithful servants, culminating in the obedience of Jesus Christ and the glory that follows surrender.

Through his writing, Peter's desire stays steadfast:

to draw hearts back to the Word,

to inspire a life of holiness and faithfulness,

and to magnify the Lamb who obeyed unto death,

so that through His obedience, we might live forever.

TABLE OF CONTENTS

PREFACE ix

INTRODUCTION xiii

Reflection and Prayer.. xv

DEDICATION xvii

CHAPTER ONE: THE OBEDIENCE OF FAITH — NOAH AND
THE CALL TO WALK WITH GOD 1

CHAPTER TWO: ABRAHAM — LEAVING ALL BEHIND 6

CHAPTER THREE: JOSEPH — OBEDIENCE IN THE PIT AND
IN THE PALACE...11

CHAPTER FOUR: MOSES — THE RELUCTANT BUT
CHOSEN SERVANT 16

CHAPTER FIVE: DAVID — A HEART THAT YIELDS................. 22

CHAPTER SIX: ISAIAH — THE CRY OF SURRENDER 27

CHAPTER SEVEN: JEREMIAH — THE TEARS OF
OBEDIENCE.. 32

CHAPTER EIGHT: DANIEL AND EZEKIEL
— OBEDIENCE IN CAPTIVITY 37

CHAPTER NINE: THE OBEDIENCE OF CHRIST
— THE SON WHO FULFILLED ALL 44

CHAPTER TEN: THE APOSTLES — OBEDIENCE THAT
TURNED THE WORLD UPSIDE DOWN 50

CHAPTER ELEVEN: PAUL — OBEDIENCE UNTO DEATH 55

CHAPTER TWELVE: THE CHURCH — THE OBEDIENCE
OF THE CALLED-OUT ONES 61

CHAPTER THIRTEEN: THE RETURN OF THE KING —
THE GLORY THAT FOLLOWS OBEDIENCE 66

CHAPTER FOURTEEN: ETERNAL REST — THE
REWARD OF THE OBEDIENT 72

FINAL REFLECTION AND PRAYER 78

ACKNOWLEDGMENTS 83

FINAL BENEDICTION.. 85

PREFACE

Obedience is the purest act of faith. It is the language through which love speaks and faith breathes. From the beginning, every man and woman who walked with God did so through the narrow path of obedience — not out of compulsion, but out of trust in the One who calls. For faith without obedience is only belief; but faith that obeys becomes transformation.

In Jesus Christ, obedience reached its highest expression. Though He was the Son of God, He entered the realm of human frailty, clothed Himself in flesh, and chose the will of the Father above His own. In Gethsemane, His humanity trembled, yet His divinity triumphed. Through His suffering, He learned obedience — not because He was disobedient, but because He embraced the full cost of submission. His obedience did not end at the cross; it was crowned in glory.

This is the divine pattern: faith gives birth to obedience; obedience is tested through suffering; perseverance sustains it; and glory is its eternal reward. Abraham, Joseph, Moses, David, the prophets, and the apostles all walked this same sacred path. Each bore the price of obedience, and each, through tears and trials, found that the will of God is not only perfect but redemptive.

The Act of Obedience is a journey through that path — from the Son who obeyed unto death, to the servants who followed in His steps. It is a call to every believer to see that obedience is not weakness, but power; not loss, but gain; not the end, but the beginning of divine glory.

The message of obedience has always carried a deep weight upon my heart. In my walk with the Lord, I have learned that obedience is not always celebrated, nor is it often understood. It requires quiet surrender when the world demands explanation, and perseverance when the cost feels too high. Yet, through every season, I have seen that God measures faith not by words spoken, but by steps taken — steps of obedience, sometimes through pain, but always toward His glory.

This book was born from moments of reflection and prayer — moments when the Spirit of God reminded me that every act of true obedience mirrors the obedience of Christ. His submission to the Father's will was not a moment of weakness but of strength; not defeat, but divine triumph. From that sacred example flows the story of every faithful servant who dared to trust God beyond understanding — Abraham who left all behind, Joseph who suffered for righteousness, Moses who faced his own inadequacy, David who bowed in repentance, the prophets who stood alone in truth, and Paul who finished his race with joy despite chains and scars.

In each of their lives, we see one golden thread: the cost of obedience and the glory that follows. The cost reveals our humanity; the glory reveals His divinity. Between the two lies the testing ground of faith — where every believer must decide whether to walk by sight or to trust the unseen hand of God.

My prayer is that as you read these pages, the Holy Spirit will awaken in you a deeper desire to obey the voice of the Lord — not reluctantly, but with love. For it is in obedience that faith becomes living, that suffering becomes meaningful, and that glory becomes inevitable.

May this book remind you that no act of obedience is ever wasted, no tear shed in surrender unseen, and no step taken in faith unrewarded. The same God who called, sustained, and glorified those who walked before us is still calling today — calling you and me to trust, to follow, and to obey.

INTRODUCTION

Obedience has always stood at the heart of man's relationship with God. From the garden of Eden to the garden of Gethsemane, the story of Scripture unfolds around one simple question: Will man trust and obey the voice of his Creator? It is the thread that runs through every covenant, every calling, every act of faith recorded in the Word of God.

Yet obedience is not merely doing what God says — it is believing that His will is perfect even when it leads through pain. It is faith proven by surrender, love expressed through submission, and hope that endures through trial. Every act of true obedience carries both a cross and a crown.

When Adam disobeyed, creation fell under the weight of rebellion. But when Christ obeyed, redemption entered the world. His obedience reversed the curse — not only through His death, but through every moment He chose the Father's will over His own. From His baptism in the Jordan to His agony in Gethsemane, Jesus' life was one continuous act of obedience. And because of His obedience, the door to glory was opened for all who would follow in His steps.

Throughout Scripture, we see this divine pattern repeated in the lives of those who walked with God. Abraham obeyed the call to leave everything familiar. Joseph obeyed in silence through years of injustice. Moses obeyed despite his fears. David obeyed through repentance. The prophets obeyed when obedience meant rejection. And the Apostle Paul obeyed when obedience cost him everything but gained him eternity.

Their stories remind us that obedience is not comfortable — it is costly. It will test the heart, confront pride, and require faith when sight offers no assurance. But it is also the path where we meet God most intimately. In the valley of obedience, faith matures; in the fire of obedience, character is refined; and in the reward of obedience, God's glory is revealed.

This devotional journey is not merely about reading their stories but about finding our own reflection within them. The call of God still echoes today — sometimes in whispers, sometimes in storms — inviting each of us to say, "Here am I, Lord, send me." It is an invitation not to comfort, but to communion; not to success, but to surrender; not to fame, but to faithfulness.

As you turn these pages, may your heart be stirred to a deeper walk of obedience — the kind that costs much but yields more; the kind that transforms the soul and glorifies God. For in every act of obedience, no matter how small or great, there lies the same pattern that marked our Savior's path: faith, suffering, perseverance, and glory.

Reflection and Prayer

Reflection

Every act of obedience begins with a whisper — a gentle nudge from the Spirit calling us to trust God's will above our own. The question is never whether God is speaking, but whether we are willing to follow. Obedience is not measured by how much we understand, but by how deeply we believe that His way is perfect. When we surrender our will, we enter into the very heart of faith — the place where heaven and earth meet in harmony.

Pause for a moment and reflect:

What has God been asking of you?

What step of obedience have you delayed, feared, or reasoned away?

Perhaps this is your time to respond, not with words, but with surrender — for every obedient heart becomes an altar where God reveals His glory.

Prayer

Heavenly Father,

Teach me to love Your will more than my own desires.

Help me to see that obedience is not bondage, but freedom — not loss, but gain.

When Your path leads through suffering, give me the strength to endure.

when it requires letting go, give me faith to trust Your goodness.

Let the obedience of Jesus Christ shape my heart and renew my mind.

May His example become my pursuit, His surrender my strength,

and His glory my ultimate reward.

I choose today to walk in Your will, even when I do not see the way,

for I know that every step of obedience brings me closer to You.

In Jesus' name,

Amen.

DEDICATION

This book is lovingly dedicated

to the One whose obedience redeemed the world —

Jesus Christ, the Lamb of God.

May every word within these pages bring glory to His name

and draw every heart nearer to the will of the Father.

And to all who choose to follow Him in faith —

who obey when the cost is high,

who trust when the path is dark,

and who endure when the world misunderstands —

this work is for you.

May you never forget that your obedience is seen,

your tears are counted,

and your reward is sure.

*"For God is not unjust to forget your work and labor of love
which you have shown toward His name."*
— Hebrews 6:10 (NKJV)

CHAPTER ONE: THE OBEDIENCE OF FAITH — NOAH AND THE CALL TO WALK WITH GOD

"Thus, Noah did; according to all that God commanded him, so he did."
— Genesis 6:22 (NKJV)

The Meaning of Obedience

Before we follow the footsteps of the men and women who obeyed God, we must first understand what obedience truly means. In Scripture, obedience is never mere compliance — it is faith in action. It is the outward expression of an inward trust in the authority and goodness of God.

In Hebrew, the word often translated as obedience is שָׁמַע (shama), which means to hear intelligently, to heed, to listen with the intent to respond. Obedience, then, begins with hearing — not just sound, but revelation. It is the heart's readiness to receive the Word of God and align one's will with His. To "hear" in the Hebrew sense is to "obey."

In the Greek New Testament, the word ὑπακοή (hypakoē) carries the same essence. It means to listen under authority — to place oneself beneath the word spoken and respond in submission. It is derived from ἀκούω (akouō), "to hear," combined with the prefix ὑπό (hypo), meaning "under." Thus, obedience in the biblical sense is not about forced submission, but willing surrender born from faith and reverence.

Theologically, obedience is the bridge between belief and transformation. One can believe in God and yet remain unchanged — but when belief produces obedience, it manifests faith that saves. James wrote,

"Faith without works is dead." — James 2:26
and Paul affirmed that the goal of the Gospel is
"Obedience to the faith among all nations."
— Romans 1:5

Obedience is not the root of salvation, but the fruit of faith. It is the evidence of a heart that trusts God enough to act upon His Word, even when the outcome is unseen. It is this kind of obedience that first appeared in the life of Noah.

Noah: The Example of Obedience in an Unbelieving World

In the days of Noah, the earth was filled with corruption and violence (Genesis 6:11). Humanity had turned from God, living by sight, not by faith. Yet amid a rebellious world, one man found grace in the eyes of the Lord (Genesis 6:8). What set Noah apart was not perfection, but obedience — faith that heard and acted.

When God spoke to Noah about the coming flood — an event never before seen — Noah believed the word of the Lord. Hebrews 11:7 records,

"By faith Noah, being divinely warned of things not yet seen, moved with godly fear, prepared an ark for the saving of his household..."

Noah's obedience was not partial or selective. Scripture emphasizes,

"Thus, Noah did; according to all that God commanded him, so he did." — *Genesis 6:22*

This repetition is divine emphasis — complete obedience. Noah did not reason with God; he responded. He obeyed despite ridicule, despite delay, and despite the impossibility of what God commanded. His obedience required decades of perseverance, faith under mockery, and steadfast work when there was no visible sign of fulfillment.

Through that obedience, Noah became the instrument of salvation for his generation — a prophetic picture of Christ, whose obedience would later bring salvation to the world. Just as Noah entered the ark through faith, Christ invites us to enter the safety of His grace through obedience of faith.

The Cost and Reward of Obedience

Noah's obedience cost him comfort, reputation, and years of labor. He built the ark not for a day, but for over a century, guided only by divine instruction. He endured misunderstanding and rejection, yet through his faithfulness, God established a covenant of mercy.

The world mocked, but God remembered Noah (Genesis 8:1). Every act of obedience, no matter how hidden, is seen and honored by God. Obedience may separate us from the world, but it also secures us in the will of God.

In Noah's story, we see the pattern that will repeat throughout this book — obedience born of faith, tested by perseverance, and rewarded by glory. What began with Noah will find its fulfillment in Christ, who obeyed perfectly even unto death.

Reflection and Prayer

Reflection

True obedience is not a momentary act but a lifestyle of listening and following God's voice, even when it costs everything. Noah's faith teaches us that to walk with God is to move against the current of the world. His obedience preserved not only his life but the destiny of generations after him.

Are we willing to obey when obedience isolates us? Are we prepared to act on the unseen Word of God when logic offers no assurance? Like Noah, every believer must choose between the comfort of the crowd and the call of the Creator.

Prayer

Lord, teach me to hear Your voice above the noise of the world.

Give me the faith of Noah — the courage to obey when others doubt,

the patience to wait when fulfillment tarries,

and the strength to persevere when obedience feels costly.

May my life become an ark of faith,

a vessel that carries Your purpose through the floods of time.

Help me to walk with You in daily surrender,

until my obedience becomes the testimony of Your grace.

In Jesus' name,

Amen.

Bridge: The Fruit and Reward of Obedience

Obedience is never without results. When a person yields to God's voice, the effects ripple through both time and eternity. Noah's obedience preserved the human race, renewed the earth, and established the covenant of mercy — proof that obedience in the world of the living brings divine preservation and blessing. Yet even such visible outcomes are only the beginning. The true reward of obedience is not measured by what we gain on earth, but by what we inherit in God.

The life of Noah reminds us that obedience is both practical and prophetic. It changes circumstances, yet its ultimate purpose reaches beyond the temporal — to reveal the faithfulness of God. Every command obeyed is a seed of divine fulfillment; every act of surrender carries within it the promise of eternal reward.

As Noah stepped out of the ark to a cleansed world, a new covenant was born — a sign of restoration after judgment. But the story of obedience did not end there. From that renewed earth, God would call another man — a man named Abram — to walk by faith, leave all behind, and become the father of nations. Through him, obedience would take on a new dimension: not only to preserve life, but to birth promise.

CHAPTER TWO:
ABRAHAM — LEAVING ALL BEHIND

"By faith Abraham obeyed when he was called to go out to the place which he would receive as an inheritance. And he went out, not knowing where he was going."
— Hebrews 11:8 (NKJV)

The Call That Tested Faith

When God first spoke to Abram, He called him to something greater than comfort, familiarity, or certainty.

"Get out of your country, from your family and from your father's house, to a land that I will show you."
— Genesis 12:1

Those words marked the beginning of a journey of faith and obedience that would alter human history. Abram's obedience was not blind—it was faith in a faithful God. He had no map, no destination, and no visible guarantee, yet he believed the unseen promise.

This is where obedience begins: at the point where faith dares to step forward without full understanding. Abram's obedience was costly — he left behind his home, his security, and everything familiar. But with every step away from Ur, he was stepping closer to destiny.

Obedience to God's call always demands separation — not merely physical distance, but spiritual distinction. To follow God fully is to loosen one's grip on everything else. Abram obeyed not because he saw, but because he trusted. His journey became the pattern of every believer's walk with God: leaving the known for the unknown, trusting the voice more than the vision.

The Covenant of Promise

As Abraham obeyed, God responded with promise:

"I will make you a great nation; I will bless you and make your name great; and you shall be a blessing."
— Genesis 12:2

The obedience of one man became the foundation of a covenant that would extend through generations, culminating in Christ Himself. Through Abraham's surrender, God established a divine order: obedience unlocks blessing, and blessing carries responsibility.

Abraham's obedience did not make him flawless, but faithful. Even when he faltered, he returned to the altar — the place of communion and submission. Each encounter with God deepened his trust and refined his obedience. By the time God tested him with Isaac, Abraham had learned that obedience to God's will is never loss, but a step toward glory.

The Test of Ultimate Obedience

In Genesis 22, Abraham faced the greatest test of obedience — the command to sacrifice Isaac, the son of promise.

"Take now your son, your only son Isaac, whom you love, and go to the land of Moriah..."
— Genesis 22:2

The very promise God gave was now being laid upon the altar. Abraham's faith had matured to the point that he no longer questioned God's motives, only trusted His nature. The Scriptures tell us,

"He concluded that God was able to raise him up, even from the dead."
— Hebrews 11:19

This is the obedience of faith perfected — surrendering not only what we have but what we've waited for. The altar becomes the meeting place of pain and purpose, where obedience and faith embrace.

When Abraham lifted the knife, heaven intervened. God provided a ram caught in the thicket, declaring,

"Do not lay your hand on the lad... for now I know that you fear God."
— Genesis 22:12

From that moment, the name of the place was called YHWH-Yireh — "The LORD Will Provide." Abraham's obedience revealed God's character: the Provider who honors faith with revelation.

The Visible Fruit and the Eternal Reward

Abraham's obedience shaped nations, birthed covenant, and became a template for faith itself. His obedience in the world of the living brought blessing, multiplication, and a name remembered for generations. Yet beyond all these earthly blessings, there awaited the true reward — the glory of eternal fellowship with God.

Jesus Himself said,

"Your father Abraham rejoiced to see My day, and he saw it and was glad."
— John 8:56

Abraham's obedience reached beyond time — into the prophetic revelation of Christ. His earthly journey became a shadow of the eternal covenant fulfilled in Jesus, the Seed through whom all nations are blessed.

Thus, we learn that obedience in this life bears fruit we can see — lives changed, promises fulfilled — but the final reward is the glory that follows: the joy of pleasing God and sharing in His eternal purpose.

Reflection and Prayer

Reflection

Abraham's life calls every believer to step beyond the boundaries of comfort into the realm of trust. His obedience teaches that faith is not proven by what we say we believe, but by what we are willing to leave behind. The full cost of obedience is not measured in possessions lost, but in self surrendered.

Ask yourself: What "land" is God calling me to leave behind? What "Isaac" have I been afraid to place on the altar? The call of God will always challenge what we love most, but it will also reveal the God who provides.

Prayer

Father of promise,

Teach me to walk by faith as Abraham did.

When You call, give me the courage to leave behind every comfort that hinders obedience.

When You test, give me the trust to lay down every Isaac upon the altar.

May my life become a testimony of faith that acts, obeys, and endures.

Help me to see beyond the cost to the crown,

beyond the test to the testimony,

beyond the sacrifice to the glory that follows.

For You are my portion, my promise, and my exceeding great reward.

In Jesus' name,

Amen.

Bridge: From Promise to Perseverance

The obedience of Abraham opened the covenantal path for generations to come. Through his faith, God established a promise that would outlive his years and shape his descendants. Yet every promise must pass through testing; every blessing must be refined through trial.

The seed of Abraham would not immediately inherit the land, but would journey through hardship — slavery, separation, and sorrow. From among his descendants, God would raise a man whose obedience would shine through suffering — a young dreamer named Joseph, whose faithfulness in the pit and in the palace would preserve the very promise God gave to Abraham.

As Abraham's obedience was marked by faith, Joseph's will be marked by perseverance — teaching us that obedience not only believes but endures until God's word is fulfilled.

CHAPTER THREE: JOSEPH — OBEDIENCE IN THE PIT AND IN THE PALACE

"But as for you, you meant evil against me; but God meant it for good, in order to bring it about as it is this day, to save many people alive."
— Genesis 50:20 (NKJV)

The Obedience That Perseveres Through Suffering

Obedience does not always lead to immediate reward. Sometimes, it leads into the very heart of pain — not as punishment, but as preparation. The life of Joseph reveals this divine paradox. He obeyed God in purity and integrity, yet found himself betrayed, enslaved, and imprisoned. Still, through every stage of his suffering, obedience became his anchor and faith his foundation.

Joseph's journey began with a dream — a divine revelation of future authority and purpose. Yet that same dream provoked jealousy among his brothers.

"Now Israel loved Joseph more than all his children... But when his brothers saw that their father loved him more... they hated him."
— Genesis 37:3–4

Jealousy turned to betrayal, and betrayal to slavery. But Joseph's obedience to God did not waver in Egypt's darkness. Whether in Potiphar's house or the prison cell, he stayed steadfast, faithful, and honest.

"The LORD was with Joseph, and he was a successful man."
— Genesis 39:2

Here lies the secret of obedient endurance: success is not defined by circumstance, but by the presence of God in the midst of trial.

Obedience Tested in Private

In Potiphar's house, Joseph faced one of the most defining tests of his faith — a test not of pain, but of temptation. Potiphar's wife sought to seduce him daily, yet Joseph's heart remained pure.

"How then can I do this great wickedness, and sin against God?"
— Genesis 39:9

His refusal to compromise cost him his position, his freedom, and his reputation. Obedience to God's moral standard often leads to misunderstanding, but Joseph chose righteousness over recognition. He lost man's favor but retained God's presence.

Even when falsely accused and thrown into prison, Scripture says,

"The LORD was with Joseph and showed him mercy."
— Genesis 39:21

In the solitude of the cell, obedience became his worship. His prison became his pulpit. And through his humility and faithfulness, God positioned him for divine promotion.

The Rise That Glorified God

After years of waiting, interpreting dreams, and being forgotten by men, God remembered Joseph.

"Then Pharaoh sent and called Joseph, and they brought him quickly out of the dungeon."
— Genesis 41:14

In a single moment, obedience that had endured years of silence was rewarded with sudden elevation. Joseph became ruler over Egypt — second only to Pharaoh — not for personal glory, but for God's redemptive purpose. His obedience preserved not only Egypt, but the entire household of Israel during famine.

When his brothers later stood before him, trembling in guilt, Joseph saw beyond their sin to God's sovereign plan:

"You meant evil against me; but God meant it for good."
— Genesis 50:20

Obedience, when tested and refined through suffering, transforms pain into purpose. The pit, the prison, and the palace were all parts of God's design — shaping Joseph into the vessel through which His covenant promise to Abraham would be preserved.

The Visible Fruit and the Eternal Reward

In the world of the living, Joseph's obedience bore tangible fruit: reconciliation, provision, and national preservation. Yet the greater reward was unseen — the fulfillment of God's covenant through his endurance. His life prefigured Christ's own obedience through suffering unto glory.

Just as Joseph was rejected by his brothers, betrayed for pieces of silver, falsely accused, yet exalted to save those who condemned him — so too was Christ. Joseph's story points us to the greater Deliverer, whose obedience opened the way to eternal redemption.

Thus, every act of obedience — even in affliction — becomes a thread in God's grand design of salvation. Obedience may be misunderstood by men, but it is never forgotten by God.

Reflection and Prayer

Reflection

Joseph teaches us that obedience is not proven by ease, but by endurance. It is in the dark seasons — when promises to seem delayed and injustice abounds — that obedience shines brightest. When God appears silent, He is not absent; He is shaping the heart to trust Him beyond sight.

Ask yourself: Am I obeying God even when obedience costs me comfort, recognition, or fairness? Can I trust His unseen hand when I am in the prison seasons of life?

Remember, the pit does not cancel the promise — it prepares you for it.

Prayer

Father,

Thank You for the example of Joseph, who obeyed You through rejection, injustice, and waiting.

Teach me to remain faithful when I do not understand,

to trust Your purpose when doors close,

and to serve You wholeheartedly wherever You place me.

May my obedience in trial become the testimony of Your grace.

Use every pit, every prison, and every pain

to prepare me for Your divine purpose.

And when my story is told,

let it reveal not my strength, but Your faithfulness.

In Jesus' name,

Amen.

Bridge: From Perseverance to Deliverance

Joseph's obedience preserved a nation and fulfilled the promise spoken to Abraham. Yet the generations that followed would soon find themselves enslaved in Egypt — a people blessed yet bound. It was in this setting that God's call would rise again, this time to a man hiding in the wilderness — Moses, whose obedience would confront kings and liberate captives.

If Joseph's obedience teaches us how to endure suffering faithfully, Moses' obedience will teach us how to face opposition courageously. For obedience not only waits in the dark; it also stands in the light and declares, "Thus says the Lord.

CHAPTER FOUR: MOSES — THE RELUCTANT BUT CHOSEN SERVANT

"Now therefore, go, and I will be with your mouth and teach you what you shall say."
— Exodus 4:12 (NKJV)

The Call in the Wilderness

Obedience often begins where self-confidence ends. Moses was once a man of position, trained in the wisdom of Egypt, strong in word and deed. Yet God could not use his strength until it was surrendered. The prince had to become a shepherd; the confident leader had to become the hesitant servant.

When God appeared to him from the burning bush on Mount Horeb, Moses' first response was not enthusiasm but fear and resistance.

"Who am I that I should go to Pharaoh?"
— Exodus 3:11

The man who once acted in zeal now trembled in inadequacy. Yet it was in that humility that God saw readiness. True obedience is not the confidence of ability but the surrender of availability.

The Lord assured him,

"I will certainly be with you."
— Exodus 3:12

Those words became the foundation of Moses' obedience — not trust in self, but trust in the presence of God.

The Reluctant Heart of Obedience

When God called Moses to speak, Moses protested his weakness:

"O my Lord, I am not eloquent... I am slow of speech and slow of tongue."
— Exodus 4:10

But God's response revealed a timeless truth about obedience:

"Who has made man's mouth? ... Now therefore, go, and I will be with your mouth and teach you what you shall say."
— Exodus 4:11–12

Obedience is not about ability; it is about surrender. God does not call the qualified — He qualifies the called.

In Moses, we see the struggle of every servant: the tension between divine calling and human limitation. His reluctance reveals our frailty; his eventual obedience reveals God's strength through it.

Even as he hesitated, God met him with grace, appointing Aaron to assist him. Yet the mission remained Moses' responsibility — to confront

Pharaoh, to demand freedom for God's people, and to trust that obedience backed by divine power would accomplish the impossible.

Obedience That Confronts Opposition

When Moses obeyed and stood before Pharaoh declaring, "Thus says the LORD God of Israel: Let My people go" (Exodus 5:1), obedience turned into confrontation. Pharaoh's heart hardened, and Israel's burden increased.

Here we learn that obedience often makes things harder before it makes them better. The path of faith may lead through resistance, but it also reveals God's power. Each plague that followed was not only a judgment on Egypt's gods but also a demonstration of divine sovereignty.

Through obedience, Moses became God's instrument of deliverance.

"Then the LORD said to Moses, 'See, I have made you as God to Pharaoh, and Aaron your brother shall be your prophet.'"
— Exodus 7:1

The servant who once feared speaking now became the voice of heaven. Obedience had transformed fear into faith, weakness into authority.

Obedience in the Wilderness

Deliverance from Egypt was not the end of Moses' obedience but the beginning. Leading a redeemed people through the wilderness tested his patience, faith, and endurance.

"So, Moses brought Israel from the Red Sea; then they went out into the Wilderness of Shur."
— Exodus 15:22

The same people who once cried for deliverance now murmured against him. Yet Moses remained faithful, interceding when they sinned, pleading when they rebelled, and standing in the gap when judgment drew near.

Obedience in leadership means carrying others' burdens without surrendering your calling. Moses' life teaches that the higher the calling, the deeper the humility required. Through every complaint and challenge, he continued to seek God's presence, saying,

"If Your Presence does not go with us, do not bring us up from here."
— *Exodus 33:15*

For Moses, obedience was not about success but intimacy. His reward was not a throne, but the presence of the God who spoke face to face with him as a friend.

Visible Fruit and Eternal Reward

In the world of the living, Moses' obedience led to the liberation of an entire nation and the revelation of God's law. His yielded life became the channel through which God's covenant was established with Israel.

Yet his ultimate reward was not found in earthly triumphs but in eternal fellowship. Centuries later, Moses would stand on another mountain — the Mount of Transfiguration — beside Elijah, beholding the glory of the Son of God (Matthew 17:3). The reluctant servant who once said, "Who am I?" now stood in glory with the "I AM."

This is the end of all obedience: the glory of communion with God.

Reflection and Prayer

Reflection

Moses' story reminds us that obedience is not born out of perfection but surrender. God calls the weak to reveal His strength, the hesitant to display His patience, and the broken to demonstrate His mercy. The call to obedience will always expose our inadequacy, but it will also reveal His sufficiency.

Ask yourself: What excuses have I given God when He called me to obey? What fears have held me back from speaking or acting in faith? Remember, the same God who called Moses from the wilderness still says, "I will be with you."

Prayer

Lord,

You are the God who calls even the reluctant and strengthens the weak.

When I doubt my worth, remind me of Your power.

When fear silences me, give me Your words.

When obedience seems too costly, help me see the freedom it brings.

Make me a vessel of deliverance for others,

a voice that carries Your truth,

and a heart that treasures Your presence more than anything else.

Teach me to walk humbly,

to speak boldly,

and to obey fully — even when I do not feel ready.

In Jesus' name,

Amen.

Bridge: From Deliverance to Devotion

Through Moses' obedience, the people of God were delivered from bondage and taught the way of holiness. Yet obedience was never meant to stop at deliverance — it was meant to lead to devotion.

From the wilderness would come a kingdom, and from the lawgiver's legacy would rise a shepherd-king. The next stage of obedience would no longer be through signs and wonders, but through worship and surrender.

As Moses obeyed to deliver a people, David would obey to lead them in devotion. His heart of obedience would teach us that the truest offering God desires is not sacrifice, but a heart yielded to His will.

CHAPTER FIVE:
DAVID — A HEART THAT YIELDS

"I have found David the son of Jesse, a man after My own heart, who will do all My will."
— Acts 13:22 (NKJV)

The Heart Behind Obedience

Obedience without the heart becomes ritual; but obedience born from love becomes worship. David's life reveals that God values not flawless performance but yielded affection. He was not chosen because he was the strongest, tallest, or most polished — but because his heart longed to please God.

When the Lord sent Samuel to anoint the next king of Israel, He said,

"For the LORD does not see as man sees; for man looks at the outward appearance, but the LORD looks at the heart."
— 1 Samuel 16:7

In David, God found not perfection but willingness. He obeyed with song in his youth and with tears in his failures. His obedience was broken, but it was genuine — and when he fell, he fell toward God, not away from Him.

This is the secret of David's obedience: a heart that always returned to the will of God, no matter how far it strayed.

Obedience in the Fields

Before he was a king, David was a shepherd. While others saw the pasture as insignificant, God saw it as training ground. It was there, among the sheep, that David learned to listen to God's voice, to protect what was entrusted to him, and to worship in solitude.

Every psalm that flowed from his heart began in those hidden places of obedience. When lions and bears threatened the flock, David fought not for fame but out of faithfulness.

"Your servant has killed both lion and bear… The LORD who delivered me from the paw of the lion and from the paw of the bear, He will deliver me."
— 1 Samuel 17:36–37

True obedience in private prepares us for public victory. Long before he faced Goliath, David had already conquered fear through faith. The battlefield only revealed what the pasture had built.

Obedience in Battle and in Waiting

When David stood before Goliath, his courage was not in himself but in the God he served.

"You come to me with a sword, with a spear, and with a javelin. But I come to you in the name of the LORD of hosts."
— 1 Samuel 17:45

Victory came not from strength, but from obedience to divine confidence. Yet even after triumph, David's greatest test was not in battle but in waiting. Anointed as king, he still served Saul — the very man who sought to kill him.

Many fail not in adversity, but in delay. David refused to seize the throne by force, declaring,

"The LORD forbid that I should do this thing... to stretch out my hand against him, seeing he is the anointed of the LORD."
— 1 Samuel 24:6

Obedience is never proven by how we rise, but by how we wait. David chose honor over ambition, restraint over revenge. His heart yielded to God's timing, trusting that what is given by God need not be taken by man.

Obedience in Repentance

Even the most devoted hearts stumble. David's sin with Bathsheba (2 Samuel 11) became a turning point — revealing that disobedience, too, can become a place of restoration when met with repentance.

When confronted by Nathan, David did not justify himself. He bowed.

"I have sinned against the LORD."
— 2 Samuel 12:13

His repentance was not shallow remorse but deep surrender. Out of that moment came Psalm 51, a song that still teaches the world the true meaning of obedience through repentance:

"Create in me a clean heart, O God,
And renew a steadfast spirit within me...
The sacrifices of God are a broken spirit,
A broken and a contrite heart—
These, O God, You will not despise."
— Psalm 51:10,17

David's obedience was refined through failure. He learned that obedience is not only about keeping commandments, but also about returning quickly when we fall. The yielded heart is the obedient heart — one that never hardens, even after correction.

The Visible Fruit and the Eternal Reward

In the world of the living, David's obedience united a divided kingdom, established worship in Israel, and prepared the foundation for the temple of God. Through his lineage came the promised Messiah — Jesus Christ, the Son of David — whose perfect obedience would redeem the world.

Yet David's truest reward was not the throne, but the presence of God.

"One thing I have desired of the LORD... That I may dwell in the house of the LORD all the days of my life."
— Psalm 27:4

His earthly reign faded, but his spiritual legacy endures forever. Obedience gave him an eternal inheritance: "the sure mercies of David" (Isaiah 55:3), fulfilled in Christ's everlasting Kingdom.

Reflection and Prayer

Reflection

David's life reminds us that obedience flows from relationship. It is not law that sustains it, but love. When obedience comes from affection, not obligation, it becomes worship.

Ask yourself: Is my obedience driven by duty or devotion? Am I quick to repent when I fall short, or do I hide behind excuses? God does not require perfection, but He desires a heart that yields quickly to His will.

Prayer

Father,

Thank You for showing me through David that obedience begins in the heart.

Teach me to serve You with gladness, to worship You in truth,

and to return to You quickly when I fail.

Let my life be marked not by pride, but by surrender —

not by ambition, but by devotion.

Make my heart tender to Your correction and quick to obey Your call.

May my obedience bring You glory and lead others into Your presence.

In Jesus' name,

Amen.

Bridge: From Devotion to Declaration

David's obedience expressed itself through worship — a yielded heart that sang even in sorrow. Yet as the kingdom of Israel grew and hearts drifted from God, He raised another kind of servant: the prophets — men called not to sing, but to speak; not to reign, but to rebuke; not to comfort, but to confront.

If David's obedience teaches us to love God wholeheartedly, the prophets' obedience will teach us to speak for God fearlessly.

From Isaiah's cry of surrender to Jeremiah's tears of anguish, the voice of obedience will now echo through the ages — calling God's people back to holiness, even at the cost of rejection and suffering.

CHAPTER SIX:
ISAIAH — THE CRY OF SURRENDER

"Also, I heard the voice of the Lord, saying:
'Whom shall I send,
And who will go for Us?'
Then I said,
'Here am I! Send me.'"
— Isaiah 6:8 (NKJV)

The Vision That Births Obedience

Every true act of obedience begins with a revelation of who God is. Before Isaiah could proclaim the Word of the Lord, he had to see the Lord.

"In the year that King Uzziah died, I saw the Lord sitting on a throne, high and lifted up, and the train of His robe filled the temple."
— Isaiah 6:1

This vision changed everything. In the presence of divine holiness, Isaiah's self-assurance melted into humility. His first response was not eagerness to serve, but awareness of his own unworthiness.

"Woe is me, for I am undone! Because I am a man of unclean lips…"
— Isaiah 6:5

Here we find the foundation of all true obedience: brokenness before holiness. Until we see God rightly, we cannot serve Him rightly. Isaiah's cry was not born of ambition, but of awe. The coal from the altar touched his lips — a symbol of cleansing grace — and only then did obedience arise from within his purified heart.

The Call That Costs Everything

When God asked, "Whom shall I send?" Isaiah's answer was immediate: "Here am I! Send me."

It was not a calculated decision, but a surrendered response. He did not ask where he would go, what he would face, or how he would succeed. His only concern was to obey the One who called.

Yet the mission he received was one of rejection, not recognition.

"Go, and tell this people:
'Keep on hearing, but do not understand;
Keep on seeing, but do not perceive.'"
— Isaiah 6:9

Obedience for Isaiah meant preaching to a people who would not listen, warning a nation that would not repent. He was called to be faithful, not successful.

This is one of the hardest truths of obedience — that sometimes, God's measure of success is not in results, but in faithfulness to the message.

Obedience That Speaks Truth in Darkness

Isaiah's obedience was not momentary; it became a lifetime of declaration. Through decades of prophetic ministry, he spoke words of judgment and hope, justice, and mercy. He confronted kings, comforted the weary, and revealed the coming Messiah more vividly than any other prophet.

He obeyed when his words were unpopular, when his warnings were ignored, and when his life was at risk. Yet through his obedience, God's redemptive plan unfolded. Isaiah saw beyond Israel's rebellion to the promise of salvation through the Suffering Servant:

"He was wounded for our transgressions,
He was bruised for our iniquities…
And by His stripes we are healed."
— Isaiah 53:5

What began with a cry of surrender became a voice of salvation. Isaiah's obedience prepared the way for Christ, the ultimate Servant who would embody perfect obedience to the Father's will.

The Visible Fruit and Eternal Reward

In the world of the living, Isaiah's obedience brought forth revelation — his words still comfort and convict hearts centuries later. His faithfulness ensured that God's promises were recorded for generations to come.

Yet the ultimate reward of Isaiah's obedience was not earthly honor but eternal glory. His vision of the Lord foreshadowed what every obedient believer will one day see — the King in His beauty.

"Your eyes will see the King in His beauty; they will see the land that is very far off."
— Isaiah 33:17

For the one who obeys, this is the final reward: not fame, not applause, but the sight of God Himself.

Reflection and Prayer

Reflection

Isaiah's surrender teaches us that obedience begins with seeing — seeing God's holiness, our own need, and His grace that cleanses and commissions. Obedience is not born out of confidence in ourselves, but out of confidence in the One who calls.

Ask yourself: Have I honestly said, "Here am I, send me"? Or have I offered God conditions before obedience? When we yield fully, God can turn even our weaknesses into His message of grace.

Prayer

Lord,

I stand before You as Isaiah did — aware of my weakness, yet willing to obey.

Cleanse my lips, purify my motives, and fill me with Your Spirit.

Send me wherever Your will requires, even when the path is hard.

Teach me to value faithfulness over recognition,

truth over comfort,

and Your glory above my own desires.

May my life echo the same cry: "Here am I, send me."

In Jesus' name,

Amen.

Bridge: From Surrender to Sorrow

Isaiah's obedience began with surrender and endured through proclamation. Yet as Israel continued in rebellion, God raised another prophet — one who would not only speak, but weep. From Isaiah's vision of glory, the story of obedience moves to Jeremiah, the prophet of tears.

If Isaiah's obedience teaches us to speak boldly, Jeremiah's will teach us to endure brokenly. His obedience would not be crowned with applause, but with anguish — revealing that obedience sometimes carries a cross of loneliness before it brings a crown of life.

CHAPTER SEVEN: JEREMIAH — THE TEARS OF OBEDIENCE

"Before I formed you in the womb, I knew you.
Before you were born, I sanctified you.
I ordained you a prophet to the nations."
— Jeremiah 1:5 (NKJV)

The Call Before Birth

Few lives illustrate divine purpose as clearly as Jeremiah's. His calling preceded his existence — formed by God's hands, chosen by His will, and appointed by His word. Before Jeremiah ever spoke, heaven had already written his assignment.

Yet when God revealed that calling, Jeremiah's first response was one of hesitation:

"Ah, Lord GOD! Behold, I cannot speak, for I am a youth."
— Jeremiah 1:6

Obedience always begins with awareness of our inadequacy. God delights to use the humble because their obedience draws strength from His presence, not their own ability.

"Do not say, 'I am a youth,' for you shall go to all to whom I send you...
Do not be afraid of their faces, for I am with you to deliver you."
— Jeremiah 1:7–8

God's promise to Jeremiah mirrors His words to Moses: "I will be with you." This is the divine assurance that transforms weakness into willingness.

The Cost of Obedience

Jeremiah's ministry was one of the most difficult in all of Scripture. He was called to proclaim judgment to a people who refused to repent. His obedience was met not with honor but with hostility. He was mocked, imprisoned, and rejected by his own nation.

Still, he obeyed. He spoke when silence would have been safer; he wept when hardness surrounded him. His obedience was soaked in sorrow, earning him the title "the weeping prophet."

"Oh, that my head were waters,
And my eyes a fountain of tears,
That I might weep day and night
For the slain of the daughter of my people!"
— Jeremiah 9:1

Jeremiah's tears were not weakness, but worship — proof that he carried God's burden for His people. True obedience often carries both the voice of truth and the heart of compassion.

Obedience Amid Rejection

At one point, overwhelmed by opposition, Jeremiah confessed:

"Then I said, 'I will not make mention of Him, nor speak anymore in His name.' But His word was in my heart like a burning fire shut up in my bones; I was weary of holding it back, and I could not."
— Jeremiah 20:9

The mark of divine calling is that obedience becomes irresistible. Even when Jeremiah wanted to quit, the Word of God within him would not allow it. His life reminds us that obedience is not sustained by determination but by divine compulsion — the Spirit of God burning within.

Though he faced betrayal, imprisonment, and loneliness, Jeremiah's obedience preserved a prophetic witness in a collapsing nation. Through him, God revealed the coming of a new covenant written not on stone, but on hearts.

"I will put My law in their minds and write it on their hearts; and I will be their God, and they shall be My people."
— Jeremiah 31:33

Even in judgment, Jeremiah's obedience pointed to redemption.

The Visible Fruit and the Eternal Reward

In the world of the living, Jeremiah saw few results. The nation still fell to Babylon; the temple was destroyed; the people went into captivity. Yet obedience is not measured by visible success but by unseen faithfulness.

Jeremiah's obedience planted seeds that would blossom long after his death — seeds of repentance, restoration, and promise. His words shaped the hearts of later generations and prepared Israel for the coming Messiah.

In eternity, Jeremiah's tears will be remembered as jewels of devotion. God records every tear shed in obedience:

"Put my tears into Your bottle.
Are they not in Your book?"
— Psalm 56:8

Those who sow in tears will indeed reap in joy.

Reflection and Prayer

Reflection

Jeremiah shows us that obedience often carries sorrow — not because God delights in pain, but because He shares His heart with those who obey Him. To truly obey is to feel what God feels: His grief over sin, His compassion for the lost, His longing for repentance.

Ask yourself: Am I willing to obey even when obedience breaks my heart? Can I bear rejection for the sake of truth? Remember — tears shed in obedience are never wasted; they water the ground for future revival.

Prayer

Lord,

You are the God who calls even in times of darkness.

Give me Jeremiah's courage to speak truth and his compassion to weep for others.

Let Your Word burn within me like fire in my bones,

so that I may never be silent when You command me to speak.

When obedience brings rejection, sustain me with Your presence.

When it brings sorrow, comfort me with Your promise.

May my tears be worship, my pain become prayer,

and my obedience bring glory to Your name.

In Jesus' name,

Amen.

Bridge: From Sorrow to Strength

Jeremiah's obedience teaches us the price of compassion — a burden carried with tears. Yet even in his lament, a quiet strength was rising. God's people, now in captivity, would need another example of obedience — one that stood unshaken in foreign lands.

From the ashes of Jerusalem, the story of obedience would continue through Ezekiel and Daniel — men who would obey not from within Israel's walls, but within Babylon's courts. Their obedience would show us that even in exile, the faithful heart still shines, and that obedience to God transcends every kingdom of man.

CHAPTER EIGHT:
DANIEL AND EZEKIEL —
OBEDIENCE IN CAPTIVITY

"But Daniel purposed in his heart that he would not defile himself."
— Daniel 1:8 (NKJV)

"Then the Spirit entered me when He spoke to me, and set me on my feet, and I heard Him who spoke to me."
— Ezekiel 2:2 (NKJV)

Faithfulness in a Foreign Land

The Babylonian captivity tested obedience like never before. The temple was destroyed, the priesthood silenced, and the people scattered in shame. Yet even in exile, God still had His witnesses — men who would not bow to idols nor compromise the truth.

Among them stood Daniel and Ezekiel, two prophets with distinct callings but one heart of obedience. Daniel served in the palace of pagan kings; Ezekiel ministered among the exiles by the river Chebar. Both obeyed God in places where obedience seemed impossible.

Their lives remind us that the presence of God is not confined to holy buildings or sacred lands. Obedience turns every place — even Babylon — into holy ground.

Daniel: The Obedience of Conviction

When Daniel was taken captive as a young man, Babylon tried to reshape his identity — new language, new culture, new name. But while the empire could change his surroundings, it could not touch his heart.

"But Daniel purposed in his heart that he would not defile himself."
— Daniel 1:8

Obedience begins with an inner decision. Daniel resolved in advance that compromise would never be an option. His refusal to eat the king's food was not about diet, but devotion — a declaration that he belonged to God, not Babylon.

God honored his faithfulness, granting favor before men and wisdom above all his peers.

"And in all matters of wisdom and understanding... he found them ten times better."
— Daniel 1:20

Daniel's obedience continued through decades of political change and personal trials. When forbidden to pray, he opened his window toward Jerusalem and knelt as he always had.

"Now when Daniel knew that the writing was signed... he knelt down on his knees three times that day."
— Daniel 6:10

Obedience does not adjust to circumstance; it stays steadfast in principle. For Daniel, prayer was not a ritual — it was loyalty to the Living God. Even the lions' den could not silence his faith.

Ezekiel: The Obedience of Vision

While Daniel stood before kings, Ezekiel stood among captives. His calling began with a vision of divine glory:

"Then I looked, and behold, a whirlwind was coming out of the north... and from the midst of it came the likeness of four living creatures."
— Ezekiel 1:4–5

In that overwhelming revelation, Ezekiel saw the same God who once dwelt in the temple now appearing in exile. This vision shattered every limitation — reminding the exiled people that God's presence cannot be contained by walls or geography.

When God commissioned him, He said:

"Son of man, I am sending you to the children of Israel, to a rebellious nation... whether they hear or whether they refuse."
— Ezekiel 2:3–5

Like Isaiah and Jeremiah, Ezekiel was called not for popularity but for faithfulness. His obedience required strange and symbolic acts — lying on one side for many days, shaving his head, eating defiled bread — each act a living prophecy. Though misunderstood, he obeyed every command with precision and reverence.

"So, I spoke to the people in the morning, and at evening my wife died; and the next morning I did as I was commanded."
— Ezekiel 24:18

That single verse reveals the depth of his obedience. Even in personal grief, Ezekiel remained faithful to his calling. Obedience that costs nothing changes nothing.

The Fruit and Reward of Obedience

In the world of the living, Daniel's obedience brought favor and influence within the greatest empire of his time. He became a voice of integrity among pagan rulers, interpreting dreams that revealed God's sovereignty over kingdoms. Through him, the Babylonian and Persian kings learned that the Most High rules over the affairs of men (Daniel 4:17).

Ezekiel's obedience, though less visible to men, sustained the faith of a broken nation. His prophecies rekindled hope among the exiles — that dry bones could live again.

"Thus says the Lord GOD to these bones: 'Surely I will cause breath to enter into you, and you shall live.'"
— Ezekiel 37:5

In both men, obedience produced restoration — Daniel revealing God's dominion, Ezekiel revealing His renewal.

Yet their ultimate reward lay beyond the walls of Babylon. Daniel was promised,

"You shall rest and will arise to your inheritance at the end of the days."
— Daniel 12:13
And Ezekiel saw the vision of a new temple and a new city where the Lord's name would be "YHWH Shammah — The LORD Is There."
(Ezekiel 48:35)

The same God who walked with them in captivity now walks with every believer in a fallen world, calling for obedience that stands firm amid compromise.

Reflection and Prayer

Reflection

Daniel and Ezekiel teach us that obedience is not limited by environment. Faithfulness to God can flourish in any place — palace or prison, freedom, or captivity. What matters is not where we stand, but whom we serve.

Ask yourself: Have I purposed in my heart, like Daniel, to remain undefiled by the world? Am I willing, like Ezekiel, to obey even when misunderstood or alone? Obedience in exile prepares us to reign in glory.

Prayer

Father,

Teach me to purpose in my heart, as Daniel did, to stay faithful in every test.

When I live among those who do not know You, let my obedience be my witness.

When obedience is misunderstood, give me Ezekiel's courage to stand firm.

Let my life proclaim that You still rule over kingdoms and hearts,

and that Your presence is never absent from Your people.

Purify my motives, strengthen my resolve, and use my obedience to reveal Your glory —

in this world and in the one to come.

In Jesus' name,

Amen.

Bridge: JOHN THE BAPTIST — THE OBEDIENT VOICE THAT PREPARED THE WAY

"As it is written in the Prophets:
'Behold, I send My messenger before Your face,
Who will prepare Your way before You.
The voice of one crying in the wilderness:
"Prepare the way of the LORD.

Make His paths straight." '"
— Mark 1:2–3 (NKJV)

From the silence of four hundred years between the Testaments, a voice arose — not from a palace or a temple, but from the wilderness. John the Baptist was that voice. He was the bridge between the law and the Gospel, between prophecy and fulfillment, between the shadows of obedience and its perfect manifestation in the Son of God.

John's birth itself was an act of divine purpose. Announced by an angel to aged parents, his life was marked from the womb as the forerunner of Christ.

"He will be great in the sight of the Lord... and he will turn many of the children of Israel to the Lord their God."
— Luke 1:15–16

While the priests of Jerusalem clung to tradition, John lived in holy separation. Clothed in camel's hair and sustained by locusts and wild honey, he obeyed the divine call to proclaim repentance. His voice pierced through centuries of spiritual slumber, crying,

"Repent, for the kingdom of heaven is at hand!"
— Matthew 3:2

Obedience led him away from comfort into consecration. His wilderness became a sanctuary of divine preparation. He baptized in the Jordan not to build followers, but to point them to the One coming after him — the Lamb of God who takes away the sin of the world.

"He must increase, but I must decrease."
— John 3:30

That single sentence captures the heart of true obedience — the willingness to become less so that Christ may be revealed more.

John's obedience cost him his freedom and his life. For speaking truth to power, he was imprisoned by Herod and later executed. Yet Jesus called him the greatest among those born of women (Matthew 11:11), for he fulfilled his calling completely — preparing the way for the obedience that would redeem all humanity.

In John, the prophetic era reached its crescendo. He stood with one foot in the Old Covenant and the other in the New, echoing the cry of Isaiah and the faith of Elijah. His obedience opened the way for the Messiah, the Word made flesh — the ultimate expression of perfect obedience.

Bridge Reflection

John the Baptist reminds us that obedience is never about recognition, but revelation. His life was short, his message simple, but his impact eternal. The obedient heart always prepares the way for God to move — in nations, in churches, and in individual lives.

Like John, we are each called to prepare the way — through repentance, through humility, through pointing others to Christ. Every act of obedience today still echoes his cry: "Make straight the way of the Lord."

Transition

The prophets spoke of Him.

The forerunner announced Him.

Now, the Son will fulfill what they foresaw.

From John's wilderness cry, the light of perfect obedience rises — the Lamb of God, who will obey unto death, even the death of the cross.

CHAPTER NINE:
THE OBEDIENCE OF CHRIST — THE SON WHO FULFILLED ALL

"And being found in appearance as a man,
He humbled Himself and became obedient to the point of death,
even the death of the cross."
— Philippians 2:8 (NKJV)

The Eternal Pattern of Obedience

From eternity past, the Son was one with the Father — equal in glory, perfect in holiness, infinite in power. Yet when the fullness of time came, He chose the path of obedience.

"Behold, I have come—
In the volume of the book, it is written of Me—
To do Your will, O God."
— Hebrews 10:7

This was no reluctant submission; it was the purest expression of divine love.

In His incarnation, the Creator became the created. The Word who spoke galaxies into existence became an infant in a manger. The One who ruled angels became the Servant of men.

Every breath of His earthly life was an act of obedience. From His submission to His earthly parents (Luke 2:51) to His obedience in baptism ("It is fitting for us to fulfill all righteousness," Matthew 3:15), Jesus proved that obedience is not weakness — it is strength surrendered to the will of God.

He obeyed not to prove His divinity, but to reveal the beauty of perfect humanity — a life completely yielded to the Father's purpose.

The Obedience That Chose the Cross

As His ministry unfolded, obedience led Him into conflict, suffering, and rejection. He healed the sick, raised the dead, and preached truth with authority, yet He was despised and rejected by those He came to save.

Still, He said,

"My food is to do the will of Him who sent Me, and to finish His work."
— John 4:34

In the garden of Gethsemane, we see the climax of His human obedience — the moment where divine will wrestled with human agony.

"Father, if it is Your will, take this cup away from Me; nevertheless, not My will, but Yours, be done."
— Luke 22:42

There, among the olive trees, the weight of the world's sin pressed upon Him. The sweat that fell like great drops of blood was the price of our redemption. Yet even in anguish, He obeyed. He chose the Father's will over His own comfort, love over ease, surrender over escape.

Obedience here became costly — and holy. It was the obedience of love strong enough to bear the wrath of God for the sake of those who had disobeyed.

The Cross: The Crown of Obedience

The path of obedience led to Calvary — the place where glory and suffering met.

There, the sinless One became sin for us (2 Corinthians 5:21).

The righteous Servant became the sacrifice.

He was silent before His accusers, obedient even as the nails pierced His hands and the thorns tore His brow.

When the mocking crowd cried, "If You are the Son of God, come down from the cross," obedience kept Him where power could have freed Him.

He stayed because love obeys to the end.

And when He cried,

"It is finished!"
— John 19:30
obedience reached its eternal triumph.

The cross was not the defeat of obedience, but its coronation. In that surrender, death was crushed, sin was silenced, and the door of glory was opened forever.

The Glory That Followed

Suffering was not the end of obedience — glory was.

"Therefore, God also has highly exalted Him and given Him the name which is above every name."
— Philippians 2:9

The same obedience that led Him to death lifted Him to the highest throne.

The crown of thorns became a crown of majesty.

The hands that were pierced now hold the keys of death and Hades.

The One who was mocked now reigns as Lord of lords and King of kings.

Through His obedience, He became the Author of eternal salvation to all who obey Him (Hebrews 5:9). What Adam lost through disobedience, Christ restored through submission.

This is the divine paradox — that the deepest humiliation produced the highest exaltation. The scars that spoke of suffering now shine as symbols of victory. Glory did not erase obedience; it fulfilled it.

And now, through Him, every act of our obedience — no matter how small, painful, or hidden — carries eternal weight. For we obey not to earn His favor, but because His obedience lives within us.

"Christ in you, the hope of glory."
— Colossians 1:27

The Eternal Pattern for Every Believer

The obedience of Christ is both our redemption and our example.

We are called to walk the same path — to obey when it's hard, to trust when it hurts, and to endure knowing that the glory to be revealed far outweighs the cost.

"For I consider that the sufferings of this present time are not worthy to be compared with the glory which shall be revealed in us."
— Romans 8:18

Every tear shed in obedience echoes His. Every cross borne in faith mirrors His.

And every act of surrender draws us nearer to His likeness.

The day will come when those who followed Him in obedience will share His glory — not because they were perfect, but because they were willing.

Reflection and Prayer

Reflection

The obedience of Christ reveals that surrender is not loss — it is transformation.

He obeyed not for reward, but for love, and His love has now made our obedience possible.

Let your heart rest in this truth: no act of obedience goes unseen by God, and no suffering endured for His will is ever wasted. Glory always outweighs the pain.

Ask yourself:

Am I willing to obey God even when obedience demands surrender?

Do I trust that His glory is greater than my present struggle?

Prayer

Father,

Thank You for the obedience of Your Son,

who chose the cross so I might share His crown.

Teach me to follow His example —

to love Your will more than my comfort,

to trust Your plan more than my understanding,

and to see Your glory beyond my suffering.

Let Christ's obedience live in me —

transforming my weakness into worship,

my pain into purpose,

and my surrender into strength.

When I stand before You,

may I be found obedient to the call You placed upon my life —

faithful to the end, as Jesus was faithful to the cross.

In His holy and exalted name,

Amen.

Bridge: From Redemption to Commission

Through His obedience, Christ accomplished redemption and revealed the glory that follows suffering. Yet His story of obedience did not end at the cross — it continues in those who follow Him.

The risen Lord, now glorified, would soon call His disciples to walk the same path — to obey, to suffer, and to proclaim. Obedience that redeemed the world would now be entrusted to those who would carry His light into the world.

From the obedience of the Son, we now move to the obedience of His servants — the Apostles, whose surrender turned persecution into proclamation, and whose obedience would carry the Gospel to the ends of the earth.

CHAPTER TEN: THE APOSTLES — OBEDIENCE THAT TURNED THE WORLD UPSIDE DOWN

"So, when they had brought them, they set them before the council. And the high priest asked them, saying,
'Did we not strictly command you not to teach in this name? And look, you have filled Jerusalem with your doctrine!'"
— Acts 5:27–28 (NKJV)

Obedience Born From Encounter

When the risen Christ appeared to His disciples after His resurrection, He did not simply restore their faith — He redefined their purpose. Once fearful men hiding behind closed doors, they became fearless witnesses filled with divine power.

"As the Father has sent Me, I also send you."
— John 20:21

This was the moment obedience took on new meaning. It was no longer about following the Master's steps from a distance but carrying His presence within them through the Holy Spirit.

Before His ascension, Jesus commanded them:

"Wait for the Promise of the Father… you shall receive power when the Holy Spirit has come upon you; and you shall be witnesses to Me."
— Acts 1:4, 8

Their first act of obedience was not preaching — it was waiting. True obedience begins in submission, not action. Only after they waited in the upper room did heaven respond with the sound of rushing wind.

The same Spirit that empowered Christ's obedience now filled His followers — transforming ordinary men into vessels of extraordinary courage.

The Obedience That Defied Fear

When persecution rose, their obedience did not waver. They were arrested, threatened, and beaten — yet their response revealed a new kind of strength:

"We ought to obey God rather than men."
— Acts 5:29

These words became the anthem of the early Church.

Peter, who once denied Jesus in fear, now preached with fire.

John, who once leaned on the Lord's chest in love, now stood boldly before enemies of the cross.

James, the first apostolic martyr, sealed his obedience with his blood.

Obedience had turned fragile disciples into fearless witnesses.

They no longer sought safety; they sought to glorify their risen Lord.

Every command of Jesus became their commission — to preach the Gospel, heal the sick, feed the hungry, forgive their persecutors, and proclaim His Kingdom to the ends of the earth.

And though many would die in that obedience, their message could not be silenced.

"Those who have turned the world upside down have come here too."
— Acts 17:6

The world called it disruption. Heaven called it obedience.

The Cost of Apostolic Obedience

Each apostle bore the marks of obedience in their own way:

- Peter, crucified upside down, not counting himself worthy to die as his Lord did.

- Andrew, preaching the cross until he was bound to one himself.

- James, slain by Herod's sword.

- John, exiled to Patmos, where obedience became revelation.

- Thomas, pierced by spears in India, still proclaiming, "My Lord and my God."

Their obedience was not born of duty, but of love — love that had seen the risen Christ and could no longer live for anything less.

They did not obey because they sought reward, but because they had already found it in Him. Their obedience became the flame that ignited the Church, spreading light into the darkness of the world.

Visible Fruit and Eternal Reward

In the world of the living, their obedience produced the birth of the Church, the writing of the Gospels, and the global spread of the Good News. Their lives fulfilled Jesus' words:

"He who believes in Me, the works that I do he will do also; and greater works than these he will do."
— John 14:12

Yet their true reward was not earthly recognition — it was eternal glory.

They entered the same joy of their Master, the One who had promised,

"If anyone serves Me, let him follow Me; and where I am, there My servant will be also."
— John 12:26

The crowns they now wear in heaven were forged from the crosses they carried on earth. Their obedience became eternal testimony that no power of man can quench the will of God.

Reflection and Prayer

Reflection

The apostles remind us that obedience is the truest proof of love. Jesus said, "If you love Me, keep My commandments." (John 14:15)

Their obedience turned suffering into glory, fear into faith, and persecution into praise.

Ask yourself: Does my obedience cost me anything?

Would I still follow if obedience required sacrifice, rejection, or loss?

True obedience is not convenient — it is costly, yet it carries eternal joy.

Prayer

Lord,

Thank You for the example of the apostles, who obeyed You unto death.

Grant me the same courage to follow You no matter the cost.

When fear tempts me to silence, fill me with Your Spirit of boldness.

When obedience feels heavy, remind me of the glory that awaits.

Let my life reflect their faith,

my actions echo their devotion,

and my heart burn with their love for You.

Make me a witness who obeys not by words, but by surrender.

In Jesus' name,

Amen.

Bridge: From Obedience Shared to Obedience Personalized

The obedience of the apostles established the Church, but God would soon raise another servant — one unlike the rest. Once a persecutor, he would become a preacher. Once proud in the law, he would be humbled by grace.

If the apostles showed us obedience through fellowship and unity, Paul would reveal obedience through personal surrender — a life fully poured out as an offering to the One he once opposed.

His obedience would span continents, endure chains, and echo through eternity — showing that even the hardest heart can become the greatest instrument when yielded to the will of God.

CHAPTER ELEVEN: PAUL — OBEDIENCE UNTO DEATH

"But I do not count my life dear to myself,
so that I may finish my race with joy,
and the ministry which I received from the Lord Jesus,
to testify to the gospel of the grace of God."
— Acts 20:24 (NKJV)

The Surrender of a Transformed Heart

When we first meet Paul, he is Saul — a man zealous for religion but blind to truth. He was obedient to tradition, but not to truth, faithful to the law, but an enemy of grace. Yet on the dusty road to Damascus, one encounter changed everything.

"Suddenly a light shone around him from heaven. Then he fell to the ground, and heard a voice saying to him,
'Saul, Saul, why are you persecuting Me?'"
— Acts 9:3–4

Those words pierced more than his ears; they shattered his pride. The persecutor became the penitent; the accuser became the ambassador.

Blinded by light, he finally saw the One he had resisted. And in that sacred moment of brokenness, his first words of true obedience were spoken:

"Lord, what do You want me to do?"
— Acts 9:6

That question defines Paul's entire life — obedience born not from fear, but from revelation. When grace opened his eyes, obedience became his vision.

The Call That Redefined His Life

Through Ananias, God revealed Paul's divine calling:

"He is a chosen vessel of Mine to bear My name before Gentiles, kings, and the children of Israel. For I will show him how many things he must suffer for My name's sake."
— Acts 9:15–16

From the very start, obedience was intertwined with suffering. The man who once inflicted pain would now endure it for the sake of Christ. His commission was not a promise of comfort but of purpose — to proclaim the Gospel where it had never been heard, no matter the cost.

And obey he did. From Jerusalem to Rome, from synagogues to prisons, Paul's steps traced a map of sacrificial love. His obedience-built churches, raised disciples, and wrote letters that still instruct the Church today.

Yet every victory was marked by trial.

"In labors more abundant, in stripes above measure, in prisons more frequently, in deaths often...

*three times I was beaten with rods; once I was stoned; three times I was
shipwrecked."*
— 2 Corinthians 11:23–25

Paul's obedience was not a path of ease but of endurance. The scars
he bore were not signs of defeat, but marks of devotion.

Obedience in Chains

Even in prison, Paul's obedience did not waver.

The same man who once traveled freely now wrote from confinement,
yet his spirit remained unchained.

"But the word of God is not chained."
— 2 Timothy 2:9

From a Roman cell, he penned words that still inspire generations:

"Rejoice in the Lord always. Again, I will say, rejoice!"
— Philippians 4:4

To the world, his circumstances seemed hopeless; to heaven, they
were holy.

Obedience had brought him to a place of stillness, where communion
replaced activity and glory outshone hardship.

In that silence, he wrote some of his most profound truths: that grace
is sufficient, that weakness reveals God's power, and that dying is gain.

*"I have learned in whatever state I am, to be content." — Philippians
4:11*
"For to me, to live is Christ, and to die is gain."
— Philippians 1:21

Paul's chains became the final altar of his obedience — the place
where faith proved stronger than fear.

The Triumph of Faithful Obedience

When the time came for his departure, Paul's words carried no regret, only peace.

"I have fought the good fight, I have finished the race, I have kept the faith.
Finally, there is laid up for me the crown of righteousness, which the Lord, the righteous Judge, will give to me on that Day."
— 2 Timothy 4:7–8

What began on the road to Damascus ended with a crown in glory.

The one who once consented to Stephen's death now joyfully faced his own — because he had come to know that obedience may cost one's life, but it gains eternity.

Paul's obedience was not about survival, but surrender, not about results, but relationship. He obeyed because he loved the One who first loved him.

And though the sword that ended his life silenced his voice on earth, his obedience still speaks — in every believer who chooses faith over fear and surrender over self.

Visible Fruit and Eternal Reward

In the world of the living, Paul's obedience changed the course of history. The Gospel reached the Gentiles, the Church found its foundation in truth, and the New Testament was enriched with letters of divine revelation.

Yet the true reward of Paul's obedience lies in eternity — the crown of righteousness, the joy of completion, and the face of the Savior he once persecuted.

He now stands among those who obeyed before him — Abraham,

Moses, David, and all who walked by faith — testifying that every act of obedience is worth the glory that follows.

"Our light affliction, which is but for a moment, is working for us a far more exceeding and eternal weight of glory."
— 2 Corinthians 4:17

Reflection and Prayer

Reflection

Paul's life reminds us that obedience may lead through storms, prisons, and loss — but it always ends in glory.

The measure of obedience is not how easy the path is, but how steadfast the heart stays.

Ask yourself: Am I willing to obey God when obedience requires endurance? Can I still say, "Lord, what do You want me to do?" when the answer costs me everything?

Remember, obedience may end in death to self, but it always begins in resurrection power.

Prayer

Father,

Thank You for the example of Your servant Paul,

whose obedience turned suffering into testimony and death into victory.

Teach me to run my race with endurance,

to finish my course with joy,

and to obey even when I do not understand the road ahead.

When obedience costs me comfort,

remind me of the eternal crown awaiting those who endure.

When I am weak, be my strength;

when I am weary, be my hope.

Let my life, like Paul's, declare:

"To live is Christ, to die is gain."

In Jesus' name,

Amen.

Bridge: From the Apostles' Example to Our Calling

Through the obedience of the apostles — and especially Paul — the Gospel spread to the ends of the earth. Their faithfulness fulfilled Christ's commission and laid the foundation for every believer's journey.

But the story of obedience does not end in history. It continues in us.

For every generation, the call stays the same: "Follow Me."

From the obedience of Christ and His apostles, we now turn to the obedience of the Church — the call that extends to every believer, in every age, to walk in faith, endure suffering, and live for the glory that follows.

CHAPTER TWELVE:
THE CHURCH — THE OBEDIENCE OF THE CALLED-OUT ONES

"Though He was a Son, yet He learned obedience by the things which He suffered.
And having been perfected, He became the author of eternal salvation to all who obey Him."
— Hebrews 5:8–9 (NKJV)

The Continuation of Christ's Obedience

The obedience of Christ did not end at the cross — it was transferred into His body, the Church. The same Spirit that empowered His submission to the Father now dwells in every believer, calling them to walk the same narrow path.

"As the Father has sent Me, I also send you."
— John 20:21

The word church (Greek: ἐκκλησία) – the called-out ones. We are not called merely to gather, but to go — to live as witnesses of His obedience in a disobedient world.

To belong to Christ is to share His mission, His suffering, and ultimately His glory.

"If anyone desires to come after Me, let him deny himself, and take up his cross daily, and follow Me."
— Luke 9:23

The Church was born in obedience — in an upper room where hearts waited, prayed, and surrendered. The fire that fell on Pentecost did not ignite excitement; it ignited obedience — a willingness to carry the Gospel to every nation, no matter the cost.

Obedience That Reflects His Glory

The early believers understood that obedience is not passive submission but active faith. They sold their possessions to care for one another, endured persecution with joy, and faced death with songs of praise.

"They departed from the presence of the council, rejoicing that they were counted worthy to suffer shame for His name."
— Acts 5:41

Their obedience turned cities into altars and prisons into pulpits. Wherever they went, the fragrance of Christ spread — sometimes through miracles, other times through martyrdom.

That same call remains today. We, the Church of the twenty-first century, are not called to comfort, but to commitment, not to admiration, but to imitation. True revival is not measured by attendance, but by obedience.

The Church shines brightest when she is most surrendered.

The Testing of the Church

Obedience will always be tested — both in individuals and in the corporate body of Christ.

When love grows cold and truth is compromised, God raises those who will still say, "Here am I."

Throughout history, every generation of believers has faced its own test:

- The early Church faced persecution from Rome.

- The Reformation faced corruption within religion.

- The modern Church faces distraction and comfort.

But the call remains unchanged: "Be holy, for I am holy." (1 Peter 1:16)

The true Church — the obedient bride of Christ — will be purified through trial.

"That He might present her to Himself a glorious church, not having spot or wrinkle... but that she should be holy and without blemish."
— Ephesians 5:27

Our obedience today is not only preparation for service; it is preparation for His coming.

The Church's Reward: Sharing His Glory

Every act of obedience draws the Church closer to her Bridegroom. The obedience that began in a manger and climaxed on a cross will culminate in a wedding — the Marriage Supper of the Lamb.

"Blessed are those who are called to the marriage supper of the Lamb!"
— Revelation 19 :9

The same Jesus who obeyed unto death will return for a Church that obeyed unto faithfulness. The glory that crowned Him will soon crown His people.

Paul wrote,

"If we endure, we shall also reign with Him."
— 2 Timothy 2:12

For now, we labor, we suffer, we endure — but soon, we will behold Him as He is. The obedience of the Church will be complete when she stands in white, radiant, and redeemed, before the throne of the Lamb.

In that moment, every tear of obedience, every sacrifice made in secret, every trial endured in faith will find its reward in His presence.

Reflection and Prayer

Reflection

The obedience of the Church is not a collective effort of human will, but the divine life of Christ lived through His people.

We are His hands to serve, His voice to proclaim, His heart to love, His feet to go.

Ask yourself:

Am I part of the obedient Church, or merely the gathered crowd?

Does my life reflect the same surrender that defined my Savior's ?

Remember — the glory that awaits the obedient far outweighs the pain that refines them.

Prayer

Lord Jesus,

Thank You for calling me into Your body, the Church.

You obeyed the Father perfectly; now live Your obedience through me.

Help me to stand firm in a world that resists Your truth.

Make me faithful in small things, steadfast in trials, and humble in service.

Purify Your Church, O Lord —

wash her with Your Word, fill her with Your Spirit,

and make her ready for the day of Your appearing.

Until that day, let our obedience reveal Your glory on earth,

as it will one day in heaven.

In Your holy name,

Amen.

Bridge: From the Church on Earth to the Church in Glory

The story of obedience that began in Eden and was fulfilled at the cross will soon culminate in eternity. The Church that obeys in the world of suffering will reign with Christ in the world of glory.

From the obedience of the Son and His servants, we now move to the final vision — the reward of obedience:

the return of the King, the defeat of evil, and the glory of the new creation.

The journey of obedience will end where it began — in the presence of God, where His will is done perfectly and His people walk forever in His light.

CHAPTER THIRTEEN: THE RETURN OF THE KING — THE GLORY THAT FOLLOWS OBEDIENCE

"Behold, He is coming with clouds, and every eye will see Him, even they who pierced Him.
And all the tribes of the earth will mourn because of Him. Even so, Amen."
— Revelation 1:7 (NKJV)

The Final Reward of Obedience

Every act of obedience throughout history has pointed to one ultimate moment — the return of the One who obeyed perfectly. From the prophets who spoke in tears to the apostles who died in faith, all awaited the same fulfillment: the day when Christ would come again in glory.

The cross revealed His suffering; the crown will reveal His sovereignty.

The first coming displayed His humility; the second will unveil His majesty.

"Then the sign of the Son of Man will appear in heaven, and then all the tribes of the earth will mourn, and they will see the Son of Man coming on the clouds of heaven with power and great glory."
— Matthew 24:30

The story of obedience began with one man's faith in a fallen world, but it ends with the Son of Man returning to redeem that world completely. Every faithful heart that endured, every obedient soul that trusted, will behold Him — not as the suffering Servant, but as the reigning King.

The Crown After the Cross

When Jesus returns, He will not come as the Lamb led to slaughter but as the Lion of the tribe of Judah. The heavens will open, and He will ride forth as Faithful and True, judging in righteousness and reigning in glory.

"Now I saw heaven opened, and behold, a white horse.
And He who sat on him was called Faithful and True, and in
righteousness He judges and makes war."
— Revelation 19 :11

The crown of thorns has long been exchanged for many crowns.

The hands once nailed in obedience now hold a scepter of authority.

The voice that cried "It is finished" now declares, "Behold, I make all things new." (Revelation 21 :5)

Every obedient saint — those who believed through tears, labored through persecution, and held faith through fire — will share in His victory.

"When the Chief Shepherd appears, you will receive the crown of glory that does not fade away."
— 1 Peter 5:4

This is the divine promise: obedience may suffer now, but it reigns forever.

The Vindication of the Faithful

Throughout the ages, the obedient have often been misunderstood, rejected, and ridiculed. Noah was mocked; Abraham was tested; Moses was opposed; the prophets were slain; and the apostles were martyred. Yet none obeyed in vain.

On that day, their faith will be vindicated.

Those who sowed in tears will reap in joy.

Those who bowed in surrender will rise in triumph.

"Then the righteous will shine forth as the sun in the kingdom of their Father."
— Matthew 13:43

Heaven will bear witness that every step of obedience — even the ones taken in darkness — was seen, remembered, and rewarded by the Lord.

There will be no more persecution, no more sorrow, no more distance between the Master and His servants.

The faithful will hear the words for which every obedient soul longs:

"Well done, good and faithful servant... enter into the joy of your Lord."
— Matthew 25:21

The New Creation — The Fulfillment of Obedience

When Christ establishes His Kingdom, obedience will no longer be a struggle — it will be our nature. The curse of sin and rebellion will be gone forever. Creation itself will be restored to harmony with the will of God.

"And I saw a new heaven and a new earth, for the first heaven and the first earth had passed away."
— Revelation 21 :1

The glory that follows obedience is not temporary; it is eternal. The faithful will dwell with God, not as servants striving to obey, but as sons and daughters perfected in His likeness.

"And they shall see His face, and His name shall be on their foreheads... and they shall reign forever and ever."
— Revelation 22 :4–5

Here, obedience reaches its ultimate completion — when the will of God is done on earth as it is in heaven, and every heart delights to do His will without resistance, without fear, and without end.

This is the joy set before us: the everlasting reward of faithful obedience — the glory that outweighs the suffering, the crown that outshines the cross.

Reflection and Prayer

Reflection

The return of Christ is not a story of fear for the faithful, but of fulfillment. Every pain endured in obedience will be answered with eternal peace. Every loss will be met with gain. Every cross carried for His sake will become a crown of glory in His presence.

The story of obedience ends where it began — in perfect fellowship with God.

But it does not truly end; it continues forever in worship, joy, and unbroken communion.

Ask yourself:

Am I living in readiness for the King's return ?

Does my obedience today reflect my hope in His coming glory?

True obedience lives with eternity in view.

Prayer

Lord Jesus,

You are the Faithful and True, the King who is coming again.

Teach me to live in holy expectation,

to obey not for earthly reward, but for Your eternal glory.

Strengthen me to endure the trials of this life

with eyes fixed on the joy that is to come.

Let my obedience today prepare me for that glorious day

when faith becomes sight and hope becomes reality.

When You appear, may I be found watching, worshiping, and ready —

not shrinking back in fear but standing in love.

For Yours is the Kingdom, the power, and the glory forever.

Amen.

Bridge: From Glory to Eternity

The return of the King is not the end of obedience — it is its perfection.

All creation will once again walk in harmony with the will of God,

and the faithful who obeyed through tears will dwell with Him in everlasting joy.

From the cross to the crown, from the call to the glory,

obedience has revealed the heart of God — love expressed through surrender.

But there remains one final reflection:

What will it mean, in eternity, to have lived a life of obedience on earth?

The last chapter will look beyond time itself — into the eternal rest and rejoicing of the obedient,

where faith becomes sight and love reigns forever.

CHAPTER FOURTEEN: ETERNAL REST — THE REWARD OF THE OBEDIENT

"Blessed are the dead who die in the Lord from now on."
"Yes," says the Spirit, "that they may rest from their labors,
and their works follow them."
— Revelation 14:13 (NKJV)

The End of Labor, the Beginning of Rest

Every journey of obedience leads here — to rest.

Not the rest of inactivity, but the rest of completion.

The rest of one who has finished the race, kept the faith, and now abides forever in the presence of God.

"There remains therefore a rest for the people of God.

*For he who has entered His rest has himself also ceased from his works
as God did from His.”*
— Hebrews 4:9–10

The story that began with struggle ends in stillness.

The striving of obedience gives way to the serenity of fulfillment.

What once required faith is now rewarded with sight.

The obedient soul, once weary from battle, now stands in peace —
not because of merit, but because of mercy. The Lamb who was slain now
welcomes His faithful ones home, saying:

“Well done, good and faithful servant.”
— Matthew 25:23

Their tears are wiped away, their trials remembered no more.

All that remains is the joy of His presence — eternal, unbroken, and
overflowing.

Rest as Reunion

Heaven is more than a destination; it is a reunion.

Every obedient heart will be reunited not only with those who believed
before, but with the God they obeyed in faith.

“And I heard a loud voice from heaven saying,
‘Behold, the tabernacle of God is with men, and He will dwell with
them, and they shall be His people.
God Himself will be with them and be their God.’”
— Revelation 21 :3

The prophets who suffered, the apostles who labored, the saints who
persevered — all will stand together in one eternal chorus.

Their obedience, once scattered across centuries, will join in perfect harmony, singing:

"Worthy is the Lamb who was slain
To receive power and riches and wisdom,
And strength and honor and glory and blessing!"
— Revelation 5 :12

Here, obedience becomes worship.

There is no more command to follow, only communion to enjoy — a fellowship unbroken by sin or sorrow.

The faith that once moved mountains will now behold the Mountain of the Lord.

The eyes that once wept in surrender will see the King in His beauty.

The hearts that once longed for home will find it — at last.

The Reward That Never Fades

The crowns of the obedient are not kept for display but cast before the throne. For in that moment of glory, even the reward is returned in worship.

"And the twenty-four elders fall down before Him who sits on the
throne... and cast their crowns before the throne, saying:
'You are worthy, O Lord, to receive glory and honor and power.'"
— Revelation 4:10–11

This is the mystery of eternal rest: the joy is endless because love is endless.

In eternity, obedience becomes delight — the heart that once struggled to submit now finds pleasure in His perfect will.

"In Your presence is fullness of joy;
At Your right hand are pleasures forevermore."
— Psalm 16:11

There, every faithful soul will understand what could never be grasped on earth — that every act of obedience, every trial endured, every tear of surrender, was preparing them for this: the joy of the Lord Himself.

The glory that follows obedience is not only to see Him, but to be like Him.

"We shall be like Him, for we shall see Him as He is."
— 1 John 3:2

Reflection and Prayer

Reflection

Eternal rest is not an end — it is the eternal beginning of life as it was meant to be.

All obedience leads here — to everlasting union with God.

There will be no more faith without sight, no more obedience through pain, no more struggle between flesh and spirit — only love perfected in glory.

Ask yourself:

Am I living today in light of eternity?

Am I obeying not for reward, but out of love for the One who waits at the finish line?

True obedience never dies — it is carried into eternity as worship.

Prayer

Father of Glory,

I thank You for the promise of eternal rest —

the place where obedience becomes joy, and faith becomes sight.

Help me to live with heaven in view,

to obey You with love now, as I will forever in glory.

When the journey feels long and the burden heavy,

remind me of the day when You will wipe away every tear.

Until that day, keep me faithful.

And when my race is run,

receive me into the rest prepared for those who love You.

In Jesus' name,

Amen.

Final Bridge: The Everlasting Echo of Obedience

The story of obedience does not end with the obedient — it ends with God.

For all obedience reflects His nature,

and every act of surrender is an echo of His eternal love.

From the first "Let there be light" to the final "It is done,"

obedience has been the heartbeat of heaven and the pathway of redemption.

Now it becomes the eternal song of the redeemed —

those who obeyed, believed, and now behold the glory that was promised.

In eternity, obedience and glory are one.

And forever, the song of the obedient will rise through the ages:

*"To Him who loved us and washed us from our sins in His own blood,
and has made us kings and priests to His God and Father —
to Him be glory and dominion forever and ever. Amen."*
— Revelation 1:5–6

FINAL REFLECTION AND PRAYER

The Everlasting Call of Obedience

The story has come full circle. From the faith of Noah to the surrender of Abraham, the perseverance of Joseph, the humility of Moses, the devotion of David, the tears of the prophets, the voice of John, the obedience of Christ, and the endurance of the apostles — one truth remains unbroken through every generation:

Obedience is the language of love.

It is not the duty of the fearful, but the desire of the faithful.

It is the sound of a heart that has heard the voice of God and answered, "Yes, Lord."

It is the seed of every revival, the strength of every saint, and the bridge between suffering and glory.

Through every season of Scripture, obedience has proven to be the thread that binds heaven and earth. It is how God reveals His will through human weakness, and how humanity is lifted into divine purpose.

To obey God is to trust that His will is wiser than our own,

that His timing is perfect even when it feels delayed,

and that His reward will far outweigh the cost.

Every act of obedience is an altar —

a place where our will dies and His will lives.

Every tear of obedience waters the seeds of glory yet to bloom.

And every obedient soul becomes a mirror reflecting the heart of Christ.

This is the call of The Act of Obedience:

To listen.

To trust.

To follow.

And to believe that even in pain, the path of obedience always leads to the presence of God.

When our stories are finished and our faith has become sight, we will understand that obedience was never loss — it was love becoming eternal life.

Prayer

Lord God Almighty,

The Author and Finisher of all obedience,

I thank You for the sacred story You have written —

from the first act of faith to the final crown of glory.

Teach me to live a life that echoes Your Son's submission,

to walk humbly in Your will, and to trust Your wisdom in every season.

When obedience costs me comfort, remind me of the cross.

When obedience feels heavy, remind me of the crown.

When obedience seems lonely, remind me that You are near.

Let my heart be as Noah's — steadfast in faith,

as Abraham's — willing to leave all behind,

as Moses' — humble before Your call,

as David's — repentant and surrendered,

as Isaiah's — pure in purpose,

as Jeremiah's — tender in tears,

as Daniel's — firm in conviction,

and as Paul's — faithful unto death.

But above all, let my heart be like Yours, Lord Jesus —

obedient to the Father, even unto death,

so that in life and in eternity, I may share in Your glory.

Let my obedience become worship,

my surrender become strength,

and my journey become testimony to Your grace.

Until I stand before You and hear those eternal words,

"Well done, good and faithful servant,"

keep me walking in The Act of Obedience.

In the name of the Lamb who was slain and now reigns forever,

Amen.

A FINAL WORD TO THE READER

Beloved of God,

If you have journeyed through these pages, you have walked the same path that every servant of God once walked — the path of obedience. You have seen that it is not an easy road, but it is the only one that leads to life.

You have followed the footsteps of the faithful — those who believed when others doubted, who stood when others fell, and who obeyed when the cost seemed too great. Yet above them all, you have beheld the obedience of Jesus Christ — the Son who surrendered everything so that we might live in the freedom of His will.

Now the story continues through you.

Every act of surrender you make, every word of truth you speak, every trial you endure with faith — all of it becomes part of the same divine tapestry. Your obedience today may seem small, but in heaven it echoes eternally.

When the world tempts you to turn back, remember Noah's faith.

When you are asked to let go, remember Abraham's trust.

When you feel forgotten, remember Joseph's endurance.

When you are afraid to speak, remember Moses' calling.

When your heart is heavy, remember David's repentance.

When you feel alone, remember Jeremiah's tears.

When you stand before compromise, remember Daniel's resolve.

When obedience costs you everything, remember Christ's cross.

And when you grow weary on the journey, lift your eyes — for the King who obeyed unto death now reigns in glory, and His reward is with Him.

May you live each day as a living testimony that obedience is not bondage, but freedom;

not loss, but love.

not sorrow, but joy made complete in His presence.

Walk in the will of God.

Rest in His promises.

And may your life — like theirs — become a holy echo of The Act of Obedience.

ACKNOWLEDGMENTS

First and foremost, I give all glory, honor, and thanksgiving to the Almighty God, the Author of life, the Giver of wisdom, and the One whose voice still calls us to walk in obedience. Without His Spirit, this book would be words without breath; but through His grace, it became a living testimony of His faithfulness.

To my Lord and Savior, Jesus Christ, whose perfect obedience opened the way for all humankind — every chapter in this book echoes Your life, Your cross, and Your glory. May You receive every praise, for You alone are worthy.

To the Holy Spirit, my Teacher, Comforter, and Guide — thank You for inspiration in the quiet hours, for revelation in study, and for reminding me that every word written must first be lived.

To every reader, pastor, and believer who has embraced this work — may this book deepen your walk with God and awaken within you a renewed desire to live in the beauty of obedience.

And finally, to all who have stood with me in ministry and intercession — thank you.

Every prayer, every word of encouragement, every unseen act of kindness has been felt and treasured. You are part of this journey, and your obedience, too, has become a testimony of God's grace.

May the same Lord who began this work in me complete His work in you —

that together we may stand before Him one day and hear those blessed words:

"Well done, good and faithful servant."

All glory to God,

Peter Lengwe

FINAL BENEDICTION

The Glory That Awaits

Beloved,

The path of obedience may at times be narrow,

and the walk of faith may often pass through the fire.

But take heart — for every flame refines,

and every trial draws you closer to the glory that is to come.

The same Christ who walked the road of suffering now walks beside you in it.

His scars are proof that pain can become purpose,

and His resurrection is proof that obedience always ends in victory.

Do not grow weary in doing good.

Do not let fear silence your faith.

Do not measure your worth by your wounds —

for even the thorns that pierce today will one day shine as crowns of glory.

Keep your eyes on Jesus —

the Author and Finisher of faith,

who for the joy set before Him endured the cross,

despising the shame,

and has now sat down at the right hand of the throne of God.

(Hebrews 12:2)

Let this truth anchor your soul:

Every act of obedience — even when unseen — is seen by God.

Every tear sown in faith will be reaped in joy.

And every heart that endures will one day hear His voice saying,

"Well done, good and faithful servant… enter into the joy of your Lord."

Walk on, child of God.

The night is passing.

The dawn of His glory draws near.

And the One who called you will finish His work in you.

"For our light affliction, which is but for a moment,
is working for us a far more exceeding and eternal weight of glory."
— 2 Corinthians 4:17 (NKJV)

To Him be glory forever and ever. Amen.

www.ingramcontent.com/pod-product-compliance
Lightning Source LLC
Chambersburg PA
CBHW021957170726
47994CB00021B/894